INTERIOR FEMME

THE TEST SITE POETRY SERIES

Claudia Keelan, University of Nevada, Las Vegas, *Series Editor*

The Test Site Poetry Series is a collaboration between the University of Nevada, Las Vegas's Black Mountain Institute, *Witness* and *The Believer,* and the University of Nevada Press. Each year, the series editor, along with an advisory board, which includes Sherwin Bitsui, Donald Revell, Sasha Steensen, and Ronaldo Wilson, will select a winner and a runner-up. The selected winners will be published by the University of Nevada Press as part of this series.

Winning books engage the perilous conditions of life in the twenty-first century, as they pertain to issues of social justice and the earth. They demonstrate an ethos that considers the human condition in inclusive love and sympathy, while offering the same in consideration with the earth.

Refugia by Kyce Bello

Riddle Field by Derek Thomas Dew

Mouth of the Earth by Sarah P. Strong

A Sybil Society by Katherine Factor

Interior Femme by Stephanie Berger

Interior Femme

POEMS

Stephanie Berger

UNIVERSITY OF NEVADA PRESS | Reno & Las Vegas

University of Nevada Press | Reno, Nevada 89557 USA
www.unpress.nevada.edu
Copyright © 2022 by Stephanie Berger

LIBRARY OF CONGRESS CATALOGING-IN-PUBLICATION DATA
Names: Berger, Stephanie (Stephanie A.), author.
Title: Interior femme : poems / Stephanie Berger.
Other titles: Test site poetry series.
Description: Reno : University of Nevada Press, [2022]
Series: The test site poetry series | Summary: "Stephanie Berger's debut poetry book, *Interior Femme*, cracks the earth open and exposes the 'woman inside.' In a sequence of poems that explores the western feminine archetype and the internal experience of femininity from multiple angles-historical, personal, ontological, social, environmental, literary, and artistic-*Interior Femme* treats its subjects-mothers, goddesses, whores, daughters, muses, and movie stars-with a lyrical complexity that offers heartbreak, laughter, comfort, and empowerment, often simultaneously" —Provided by publisher.
Identifiers: LCCN 2021041599 | ISBN 9781647790387 (paperback) | ISBN 9781647790394 (ebook)
Subjects: LCSH: Femininity—Poetry. | Women—Poetry. | LCGFT: Poetry.
Classification: LCC PS3602.E75449 I58 2022 | DDC 811/.6—dc23
LC record available at https://lccn.loc.gov/2021041599

The paper used in this book meets the requirements of American National Standard for Information Sciences—Permanence of Paper for Printed Library Materials, ANSI/NISO Z39.48-1992 (R2002).

FIRST PRINTING

Manufactured in the United States of America

For my mother,

Chandra Mukerji

Contents

INTERIOR FEMME

Foreword

In this text, seated precisely
at the nexus of death &
the arbitrary, I find myself
in a cemetery, fluent in French.

Here, my secrets sound
more beautiful & my body
is no more than a souvenir
to its soul, a cartoon in a gold

dress grown over by brambles
& a smooth, enigmatic question.
What is the difference between a
golden Hollywood goddess & a quiet

mousy pin-up girl from San Diego,
where a wind once ripped her dress
right off & tossed her like a
slip across the country?

The answers in copper, mold or
moss, turning everything green
on another coast, my grandmother's
grave, embraced by an overgrown

echo, I was too young to understand
then why a sadness took
my mother to the movies one day
& never brought her home.

Prelude in the Key to Everlasting Life

She had only two subjects: death
& domesticity, petroglyphs & perfume,

hummingbirds & butterflies &
dragonflies in flight. It is

a miracle they never collide!
Anemically collecting dinner

bells, she had a weakness
for crystal objects & a horror

of those who collected only
the unbreakable. In *Purple & Fine*

Women, Saltus supplies
a very fine description of what

I was like then. A gay contralto
outbreak enters your ear:

a hostess, by definition,
makes no mistakes. I am

learning to sit with the weight
of a hummingbird at the table,

conversation tossed about
like an avocado, while I think mostly

about bells & optimization, how to
maximize my collection, & what

I'm getting out of it: dark
wings. She kept them beating

above her eyes like a flirt,
or a drummer with a humming-

bird heart, or a surgeon. But
if I remove it, where will I find

the rhythm to quiver as I pour
a little olive oil in the hole

where the heart used to be, select
a salt? To be clear, in this scenario,

there is no death, only survival
of the beautiful. In *Metamorphosis*,

Ovid provides a very good description
of this predicament. Ambition

like a see-saw, like a crystal
bell, teetering on the shelf

in the canyon where you must listen
to the blood of the earth before

you are allowed to see her.
There is a spring at the bottom

of the canyon where I keep my
body. There is a pit at the bottom

of the kitchen sink, available
for discovery. It is possible

to breathe both air & water.
It is difficult to breathe

both fire & earth. Imagine
all that heat & crystal

moving in your lungs. All that
mother, vinegar & salt.

Just to Give You an Idea

Imagine this rock here
is the center of the universe.

Imagine this rock is your belly button.
Divide your body into halves, then quarters,

& then: make a planet. This leg
of our journey will take about five million years.

I would love to stop & show you why
along the way, but the bones, they're telling us

to keep moving. Seas of femurs, pools
of pelvises, arranged as arrows

& symmetrical suns. Here you find a hole
& make something in it. Your aesthetics reflect

a fear of empty space, a terror of the vacuum,
like a sleeping feline with the face of an owl

& the tail of a snake must be sacrificed.
I returned to the fetal position in the afterlife.

My soul made a circular journey down the river
& up the Milky Way. Now I'm back!

So, let me tell you a little something about caves
& rivers. No one shall pass through but by me.

My belly button is the center of this universe,
a sacred valley, surrounded by mountains

filled with silver so luxuriously. We all
want to look a little richer than we are.

Those ear plugs are a status symbol.
We all know that baby alpaca is cool

to the touch, that eucalyptus towers above the peaks
& helps us breathe at the site where we can see

the founder of the lightning bolt, that golden
idol with a hole where her heart should be.

A mole on her face in the shape of
Jesus with a guinea pig laid out on the

table, Mother Mary with coca leaves
puffing out her cheeks, teenage girls

grinding the corn like teeth. I believe in
reciprocity: offering my tears & receiving

your laugh, splitting my body into two
& giving you half. This is the point

where our two valleys meet.
That's why we're in a wind tunnel.

Preface to This Edition at Dusk

Like a canyon, she opened up gradually
to the possibility of beauty in a city
throttled by bodies in the hearse around
the corner & in the stained-glass

windows of the church across
the street, the one with the buzzing
lights, nearly as haunted & magnetic
to moths as my white childhood

blanket by the sea in California,
where the tree outside my window
at night used to nestle so loudly,
I thought it was a garbage truck, so

I'd lie down in the sea without fear
or hunger, safe in a dream & present
in the pleasure of its terra cotta
feast. As she opened her eyes

to the garbage on Brooklyn's ghostly
streets at dusk, it took what I can only
describe as a "Thora Birch vibe,"
American & beautiful, angry but whimsical,

like you might die of angst, but not
before throttling the planet with a single
strand of your blue hair. If I hadn't known
how to trick my Macbook into operating

under an entirely other system, I might be
worried about keeping my body alive
too. I read the Reddit thread about
the integration problem between

Apple's browser & New York State's
Department of Labor website & as
I ran the code I wrote to keep
the page from timing out & it *worked*,

I felt a sense of satisfaction, not only
because I solved a problem,
but I understood it, inside & out,
as institutional. Still, under the weight

of so much death, "satisfaction" was mostly
just a song & "integration" was less
an illusory notion of civil victory than
an application's friendliness towards other

applications, signifying alliances between
the corporations who made them & who,
despite not actually *being* people, *were* mostly
made of people back then, just as the earth

is not an ocean, but zooming out, it is
indeed mostly an ocean—at least for now.
In short, you can take nearly any notion
out of context & create something almost

entirely other, but if it is beautiful, many
will believe it. Such is the power
of beauty. It doesn't take a genius
to give yourself a leg up & hop

that barbed-wire fence, ripping your top
off but earning for your efforts
two backstage all-access passes to
the world. Three months ago, I watched

a Youtube video by a mathematician
about exponential growth & instantly
became the least attractive version
of myself. *Did I hope to die?*

Perhaps I did want to stop, abandon
my body for once, & ascend, realizing
that tree I used to hear was her &
furthermore, she was the canyon.

It Doesn't Hurt That She Is Beautiful

As she descends into the canyon, she becomes
the descent, the way an action
can become solid as a steeple.

I can be the downfall of man!
That sunburst of flesh! For I am
the moment the desert meets water
from the mountains, an instant
connection, a language that can travel
into your memories
like a fiction, like water
from the earth, a landscape
more various than the human heart.

But she isn't human. The way her nose
came down the center
of her face like a coin, like candle
wax, a waterfall. A beautiful
creator. A dutiful daughter.
Excitedly, she babbled, more
adorable than any brook.

Things come to a head.
They come into it. You reach
a point in your life. There is a point
in every life at which
you can see no further, a black
hole in a bucket, & so you let it
drip, clear as a window
in the water. It is
important to remember
there are windows in the water.

As If I Hadn't Just Undressed Inside Her

In the bathtub, of course
I'm in the bathtub
practically asleep
with the water
like bedsheets, twisted up
until I am a great big knot,
a lie made of linen—the sum
of each small stitch.
I am developing a pattern
on the surface, I sense
a dead fish, its fleeting
life, having known only
this world of sea & land
was the mystery. My mother
in the kitchen with
hips like canyons
bringing new bread
into the world. In
the bathtub, I welcome
sailors home. I speak
a language only porcelain
knows. Her thighs
like two coasts, she pretends
to be shy. She pretends
she doesn't understand
she is a woman. Weeping
like a child for anyone
who will listen, for strangers
who are dying, I am cotton
in the morning & the tombstones
line up badly like teeth
in my bassinet mouth,
as the future circles
just above.

Tossed to the Sky to Commemorate Her Death

As she pulls herself away from the water
& the heavens descend, black
as widows, to keep me here, or
drive her away

in a chariot, I think
of our daughter, who inherited
her father's firmamental
majesty & his power

to awake with the consciousness
of being in love, to flourish,
be verdant, crowned
with ivy & joyous

& off to build a foundation, one
big bed of fertility
& war to lie in
with his lovers.

I just love him. I don't
know what to say.
If he wants a drink,
I have water.

If he doesn't like to drink, I don't
have any water, not even
in my body, I'm a goddess
& for him, I bolt across the sky.

Casting a Memory into the Cliff

Where there is a god, there is a woman
& a rock, upon which the word instruct
has been carved. Where there
is a god, there is a memory
trying not to lose itself to the man
standing before her. Where
there is a daughter, there is a father
who is a phenomenon, thirty million
& three chins, ferreting Russian sables
for favors, & there is a notebook
given to her by a former lover, where
there is an ambitious beauty & the art
all around her feet in the rocks
is ugly beside him. Where there is a man
beside himself with trepidation & a woman
with joy, I don't know who, or where
there is a shelf in the canyon, but place
yourself beside another life like
a book, like so many figurines. Stop
& stand there. You look lovely in the rain.

From What Abyss of Memory

We made no bones about ourselves
during those séances in the stacks, the back
& forth of it. "Hop a plane!" I said. Better yet,
grab a Pegasus & get over here, where
I am up a tree over you, fugaciously & with a hint
of terror, chain me to a rock, & get over here, strip me
from what abyss of memory I dragged
the phrase the oracle can only know, but
your beauty does seem to belong to a civilization
greater than my own, more effective
in accomplishing its goals. You fumbled
around & around in my pockets for
an identity, but writing a book is just
like having a baby! Any interruption
of the gestational period is at a cost
to the child. Can I be a mother?
Will it be enough?

Preface to This Edition at Daybreak

In this version, a giant yellow monarch
takes to the sky, as the seawalls

go up & the water rushes down
her thigh. In the futility of trying to be

fine, our lady of the immaculate
conversation floods the city

with a single word, burns it down
with a vowel. To be clear

she is not me, nor am I
her & this isn't a reality. It is simply

a scenario to consider. In this
edition, she has three subjects:

fur—specifically sable, ermine, &
chinchilla. In *Lady Windermere's*

Fan, Wilde understands
these nuances of a personality as

a privilege one never earns.
Still, I'm glad we had dinner,

for tomorrow she must starve. I have
sat too long at many tables with this

woman, weaving letters to her lovers
in the epistolary air, like a dragonfly.

With an obscene & unnatural thinness,
she removes inches from her waist

through sheer insanity. As I disappear,
I always wondered if somewhere

the fruits of my labor are ripe
for the taking, but I know it is tough

to find a temperate climate, let alone
live in it. It is difficult to find your way

back to the house when you sit
with your back turned to it. I was there

in that room where she would live
out her martyrdom, where a devoted

coterie of monkeys once in a blue
moon would carry her in her armchair

to the church, where she would take
her lovers, awe-inspiringly

religious, the heroine of many
a strange story, unlikely as being

chased up a hill by a rattlesnake,
but still—worth considering.

Embrace the lying child
within. She has the curse.

Before the Cold Bite of a Rattler

Sometimes, like a spoiled child, she would rot
from the inside. The wind, offering nothing
but a silent treatment of the drapes, the sun & copper
earth.
       She walked across the lava with a familiar
rhythm, finally snapping, like
                     a discharged soldier
walking with a cane when he no longer needs
one. More than a mystery, she was a mood, a ring
on her most important finger symbolizing nothing
but desire
       to glitter. In *Poetry & the Imagination,*
Emerson insists a good symbol is the greatest
argument, more persuasive than any evidence
to its contrary.
             The value of a lie is that you
are a lie. The glaciers & ice caps you think you
understand until they are melted down
to the woman
          inside. Try to melt that woman & you'll lose
the laurels that disguise your baldness.
                   Learning
to use his mouth as your own is the most difficult. The
ethereal chasing the unspeakable. Flying squirrels
hiding in foxholes. Pressing charges like linens.
The end isn't the point & yet it is indispensable.

Introduction to the Mother

She believed in everything & I
believed in nothing, or vice
versa: prodigal, patented & perfumed.

People go mad. Others kill themselves.
Some fall in love. She was one of the latter.
She *believed* in everything, but she *knew*

that for her there was only one fate: to fall
in the water, come up with nine daughters,
& drift down the river for a century

like a myth. When she returned to the
spring from which she had sprung
like so much water before her,

what were you doing? Or, rather,
what have you not been doing
all this time, since the beginning,

when the abyss parted her
lips & the sky & the earth fell
into each other's arms?

I was rhyming the universe
with *"le coup de foudre"* &
overthrown by electricity.

In the droop of her lips, there
was France itself, but this child
was the new Rome.

Say "Bonjour" to the Memory, Our Guest

She has been haunting my body for years
like the stacks of an archive
                        inflammable
filling it up with ghosts by the pail
translucent fluids in large buckets
                        Meanwhile
I have served her my canvasback over & over
bailed my love into her burning barn, dressed
with a cavernous absence of smarts, in the dark
she looked upon some great vista, visible only to
her fingers closed around the perfume of my wrist,
                        visible only to you, my body
this garment, incapable of revision, our bedroom,
its ornaments & amber spirits, mahogany
                        ghosts, she
is dosing me with her little "lost in memories,
tossed into death" mnemonic mantra, but death
is a little different—
                        its whisper
is monosyllabic, memory
raises the latch: "I've birthed nine girls!" she cries, each
is just a part of the landscape now. I am here in front of you. I
                        am completely blue, my arms
& legs raised in little notches, put your tongue inside, drink
from the bruising, the spring of her lips, you'll remember: we
are human,
we rhyme.

Interlude in a Lost Key

As if the last cool breath of fall
had swelled into a bead
that dropped thirty degrees
in an evening, our mistress
lay as torpid as that cold.
She was a woman whose 21st birthday
would never be fêted again.
It should be added that had she been
bald, she would have been no starlet
but on most days her perennial
locks, bright & fragrant as rosewood,
descended from her head as if
they were two branches
of an imperial staircase.
This was not one of those days.

Memory with the Beautiful Hair

Is it love or death that rouges
the mulberry bush? Only
the lovers can know what goes on
between them, a redwood grows.
It is certainly not red, she moaned
as a child, it is molten
copper, but into the core
of that fantasy, perplexity came.
She knew her hair was a garland
of flame, supernally lovely, elevated
rhyme to the dignity of sport
with her retort, but that is another lyre
altogether & the phonograph
in my throat only plays
the songs I like to remember.
They are very lovely, your pictures
of the sacred peacocks, the vainest
of all birds, & sometimes
when I really like a man, I lie.

A Beautiful Boyish Insouciance

In an earlier volume, everything tough
was a nail & that was it before the flood
came. Remember when I had my aura read
in the street on a sunny fall day & it spilled
into a pool of silver & lavender & turquoise

& the woman hugged me & asked us
for cigarettes? That was this morning.
Do you remember the morning? Losing
the cargo, the slippage, a masquerading
planet became tame. She had never been.

We'd never & I couldn't keep sipping on
the sip cup. "You can't keep me in the slips
like this!" I cried. *You can't keep me here!*
& there, mounted like a flame, her delight
in the dream of possessing this man.

It promenaded straight without care
into the domain of beauty, which
does not sleep, but lies awake at night,
dreaming with eyes open. Those eyes.
When she chose, she could flood them

with languors, sublimate Paris into
a tropic frame, wet, trenchant, bellicose,
pugnacious, but never frowzy. The
melting measures proceeded & the
ice in her stare gave way to steam.

It was as if she had dropped a curtain.
My body holds a heart that cannot love.
It holds another heart that cannot help
but love. They are conjoined twins &
all in black. Sometimes I want to enter

your body too, penetrate the surface with
the most engorged part of my soul, place it
inside you. I am the man here, cerebral &
happy, bad & abroad, bored & supportive,
watching these women, who are always

walking by in their bodies, but I hate
to boil it down to oversimplification.
I would love to be focused, honest,
& hard-working, but I can't do anything.
Not today. I am too far away from the planet.

Excuses fly like birds, & I saw them flying
in your eyes. Literally. You stared into my
eyes & I saw birds. But it's not like it was
an intensely emotional experience. I'll admit—
before the flood, it was a nice morning.

Boots & That Which Suits a Goddess

I am so tired of bracelets &
cajoleries, when he came
to me in that shack
of a meadow, my heart.

I say to myself now, "I
am crossing a bridge, it is
frozen. Snow takes its place
in my shoes, they are broken."
It was happening to me, far off
to that one woman, horrible
because she opened a path
to the ruin; a sudden & necessary
tenderness toward her, she
who is not queen & walks there.

It does not suit me to pretend
that the snow comes in through
my shoes when he is dancing with
me & his hand on my waist
makes a strong impression.

It's only a dream, but as a hand,
it sticks & works its way into
my wakefulness & there you are
again, the love of my life, great
God of Olympus, overwhelming
me: you are winning.

He beats me & I love him. I don't
know if I love him, but I let him
think he is beating me. I
am being punished for
this language, but who

knows whether it's a man, an
angry muse, or a solitude
there. It does not suit me
to pretend I am being beaten.

Sexual Misconduct

Excuse me, are you curious George's father?

                                                               I'm afraid.

The uncle?

                                 You have the wrong girl.

      Certainly.
      I'm little curiosity.

                          Have or are?

Half or wrong?

                22 years old.

I have difficulty speaking the language but understand it perfectly.
There's a market for that on the Internet.
Had I stopped I might have moved in some other direction.
                              Half or wrong?
                          Right & left I can deal with.
What about north & south?
Too tied up with the up & down.
                In this culture.
                    Makes a girl sea-sick, a little more consistent.
Can I have a cigarette?
            You have one in your hand.
Do you want the panties or not?
            You have the wrong girl.
Has anyone ever told you those things will kill you?
                That's not a question.
79 years old.
My father was a sociologist.
      Too tied up with the up & down.
He appreciated fine wood-working.
I believe he hated the French.
      I'm afraid.
      I have difficulty speaking the language but understand it perfectly.
                In this culture.
            I was eight & nine when I lived there.
He kept a wooden fisherman out on the deck.

He showed little interest in metals.

I like your mustache.

Certainly.

I like your hook.

You have one in your hand.

Yes, less to lose.

Have you ever felt such shimmering exhaustion?

She bet me she couldn't sit on my stomach for an hour without my
crying uncle.

There's a market for that on the Internet.

The uncle?

Do you want the panties or not?

My father was a sociologist.

That's not a question.

In this culture.

Excuse me, are you curious George's father?

Had I stopped I might have moved in some other direction.

But I've little curiosity.

Have or are?

22 years old.

Perhaps it is better to walk around in a bubble.

Yes, less to lose.

Less to emboss.

Maybe more to enamel.

He showed little interest in metals.

Half or wrong?

I'm afraid.

Right & left I can deal with.

Can or have?

Can I have a cigarette?

I can be the wrong girl.

29

I Am Trying to Ground You
& Have Been All Along

Located somewhere between
Manhattan & the Chesapeake
Bay cement transporter docked

in Brooklyn, a top-hat pirouettes
in an eddy of sunlight & the water
slaps itself clumsily against anything

that will stand for it, like a teenage
boy in the Hollywood hills
in a silent film because young

women don't actually stand for that
kind of consensually murky romance
anymore & in this world will probably

become physically intimate with men
less & less, the old wolves grinning
at the edges of the docks, revealing

something slightly more savory even
than the heritage pork chops my mother
shipped overnight wrapped in brambles

& a bay leaf & anise-infused
brine recipe, as if life were still
sumptuous & this pause were just

an opportunity to marinate, a subject
upon which chefs, I'll remind you, tend
to have wildly divergent viewpoints.

Is it worth it to compromise one's
identity in order to transcend the
limits of nature? In another world,

I keep my daughters in a glass jar
filled with knowledge & berries
because boys will be boysenberries

& they will try to take you to that
mountain-palace I could never enter.
My head wouldn't fit through the door.

Merciless Palace to Remember

What is the point of a memory
palace if I hang her portrait in every
room? As one might stuff a man
made of paper with more
paper so that he can burn
longer, I posit that it helps me
remember. The desert room,
where I hung a candelabra
from the sky & the weight
of it was nothing to a man
like that. In every room
she kept the tape for measuring
mercilessly my shortcomings
& with luxurious scorn, wondered
how she had ensnared me there.

Even I, Who Have No Lover, Love

Bitter & jealous as a demi-
goddess, she pours from herself the
nectar of her being, becomes a vessel
for children, the bitch in the sun.
She is statuesque. I know my devotion
is difficult to understand—so too
is the language she speaks. Nothing
could stop me from kissing her cheeks
again & again, wearing away at the
stone, but soon they are sunken,
so warped that when she falls
asleep on her side, moisture
collects there in a small pool
that we can drink from.

In the Star's Own Words

To reject motherhood
would be to be caught, panther
in the conservatory,
prince at the gallows, six of one
half a dozen of those aesthete cameos,
nose like a chili, to be rubbed
all fiery & red, all wisps of hair
ivory on black on blue around the lips
like the lip of a porcelain cup.

I drank. I was that girl,
a reproduction of the others,
one of nine, a lady
of the night, a real *viveur*.

My word, how did you feel?

Sunstruck! at first,
or some shadow of such.

The Graveyard

I have begun to see voices in the fruit aisle.
    I have emptied myself like a bucket of ghosts!
So why do you welcome them?
       If life moved us.
          As a van jam-packed with melancholy cops.
      From the city to the country.
    From the fiery blue underbelly of a matchless flame.
            We would suck cigars.
   Feel absolutely forbidden to open the door to the grassy area.
If I spoke very quietly.
   I'd see you.
Never say you see someone.
   I have begun to see voices in the fruit aisle.
Better, more often.
        You'd hear yourself yelling.
         From the city to the country.
        We spend all this time laughing.
        Wait, do we?
If I spoke very quietly.
   Like a fiddle or a wool heart.
    Several blue strands fall out in her hands.
Never say you see someone.
     I'm looking for my angle face to keep me warm this winter.
     I'm looking for invisibility.
You'd hear yourself yelling.
   I have emptied myself like a bucket of ghosts!
Like a fiddle or a wool heart.
     I like ankles knees thighs groin tummy tits, especially tits.
   Every angle's terrible.
     From the city to the country.
  True.
As a van jam-packed with melancholy cops.
   I'd see you.
Better, more often.
   We would suck cigars.

Why hello, speckly sparrow-like bird!
So why do you welcome them?
He isn't bad-looking.
As a van jam-packed with melancholy cops.
From the fiery blue underbelly of a matchless flame.
I like ankles, especially ankles.
He isn't bad-looking.
If I spoke very quietly.
Better, more often.
If life moved us.
Like a fiddle or a wool heart.
Every angle's terrible.
So why do you welcome them?
Wait, do we?
Feel absolutely forbidden to the open door to the grassy area?
We spend all this time laughing.
Better, more often.
We spend all this time laughing.
Wait, do we?
I'm looking for my angle face to keep me warm this winter.
Several blue strands fall out in her hands.
From the fiery blue underbelly of a matchless flame.
I like angles, especially angles.
Like a fiddle or a wool heart.
I'm looking for invisibility.
Why hello, speckly sparrow-like bird!
Never say you see someone.
Wait, do we?
We would suck cigars.
True.
I'd see you.
True.
From the city to the country.
Better, more often.

Everything Tastes of Licorice If You Let It

In the warm shade of a subtle tree & a sense
of never-ending fatigue, she slipped into

a world without hinges. Every door
slumped against its molding, the tomb's gate

lay on the lawn like a lover, the moon
at the bottom of a very deep hole, a body

mirrored in the water without flaws,
& in a grand display of discontinuity,

the fault lines in her lips blurred
in pixelated bliss. A gravestone

is indestructible not to symbolize
some eternal spirit but because

she is no longer fragile. Suffering
belongs only to her daughters, a lineage

of pain traveling back so far, the patina
at the edges of our eyes starts to show.

Begging to be touched are the roots
of the touch-me-not, whose foliage speaks

in a language that folds inward. It cannot hear
the wind bristling its skin as the grass comes up

in gigabytes. I have trademarked this digital brand
of mystical bucolia. I call it "mathemagical"

because there is a bone in my body that is silly
& tasteless & tawdry & set like a death mask.

At the flashpoint between glee & horror,
the little-leaf linden gives Lady Lazurus a hug

& a bone made of science springs forth
through her skin, where so many doves

have suddenly converged. In Antwerp, a library
sprouts behind closed doors, & on screen

in a golden glow, she starts a little show
in which an orange-bellied robin, waddling along

Persimmon Path, turns & hops through the grass
towards the tomb of Leonard Bernstein, while

Basquiat basks in the colors that surround
his indestructible solitude. In paintings,

we still gather like players on stage
even though the show is fire & the house

goes up in flames. To excite the blaze,
she & I wear masks. We hold doors open

like gentlemen & suddenly cracking open
a tortoiseshell fan, I notice the hinges

are back. I place a candle over the little hole.
It's the shadows that I came for after all.

In Paintings We Appear in Forests in Threes

The verdict distributed its measures
throughout the chambers
of her house like a waltz
& in my heart, I wanted to
dance to the sentence:
                    Courage,
Madame. Everything shall be taken
from you—your daughters, your kingdom,
your palace & riches, the dreams
& illusions of your girlhood. Your freedom
cannot console you now.
                    Now I grow old
& I seem to grow paler & by the shade
in the hollow I forget your name.
Unbearably beneath the falling
leaves, she offers to draw me
a circle with her untrained
hand, & the earth stops
to be given its form.
                    A daughter
presents a meditation on death
& domesticity, rape & memory,
presents you with a partition
between & on it,
                    a portrait
of your world. There are women
in the picture whose names you
will never know. I am present
with them & still dancing, as
with so many daughters
buried in the paint beneath
the gazebo of sheets.

My Mandolin

I was fifteen when I found my mandolin, my little boy, an orgy for
the traces. I cannot sleep alone without you, my Lord. I cannot sleep.
Give me just one moment please to weave this particularly magenta
piece of yarn through our story. Is the bed slipping from the bed? The
couch from the couch? I can't tell, my mandolin, tell me in song. If we
could take this outside, please. Yes, my Lord. Come see the moon. It
is not expensive. Come pull the strings on my mandolin, little boy, my
mandolin, an orgy for the couches who listen at windows. Everyone
eating bread in the night, tracing the music in the air, tasting this
particularly magenta-colored piece of yarn, flour on their faces, a cool
breeze on their faces. A regatta of messenger birds mob my mandolin,
my mandolin, a plot of traces, the water in our faces, the wings, my
Lord, they loom, my mandolin, my mandolin.

Below His Monocle

Before the pharmacy, above the apothecary,
I lived for a spell. With broomsticks
in a closet with no name.

Along the spine of the hill, below the ashen face
of heaven, I waited for his ovine spirit
to graze my face.

She held her breath so tightly it escaped her, she lay
in the desert, like it's just so cruciform
to grace the vultures sitting down for dinner with

gods, like gentlemen in comparison,
cartoonish only to the stars, the rhyme
of her cracked lips.

It is everywhere, this sack
of pronouns, holding onto each other for dear
life—its fetching beaks & blouses, boutonnières. It is dear

to glare imperially, from one's mountain-palace.
If vulgar, it is vulture, valiant, a peach
& so chatty, she inhaled the stone voluptuously

with a church-like desire to conceal
her meaning. The tremendous gentleness
of that gesture smothers me, divested of its

daughters, its laurels, its flesh, the page
holding itself together
like a life.

The Past Is Not the Past

In the swirling morning after, I discovered her
smile quite eerily at the bottom of my cappuccino,

her freckles in every speck of cardamom dusting
my pistachio muffin, & in the mirror

of the powder room, tiny massacres
in her eyes. Yesterday, I wrote a song

that I will sing tomorrow, fat as lady with
a piano in her pants & beneath a rock, I

discovered the key to a door that I will open
in order to leave. Do you hear that? The truth

just sounds different. Considering the
future adds a certain dimension. We lived

for a while in a dirty love nest, constructed
of feathers & fallen branches. I returned years

later & the furniture was expensive, beautifully
beveled, carefully crafted, curated & I knew

the disorder was my own. I could see myself
in the baking pans. I held one up to my face

as I left & bequeathed a small streak. No longer
could she rest on the laurels of her dumbness.

Learning, at first, does feel like a loss.
Occasionally she would let go by

some misogynistic half-baked truth
launched from the mercurial knee-jerk

of the patriarchy. Later, she wrote
a terrible Yelp review for our society

in general. Consumed for hours, literally
feasted upon by her imagination. Spirit

mouths caressing her body ominously.
Violated even in her dreams, but also in his.

It isn't enough to face this fact. It's a disease
you have to battle like a knight. The sky

is sick, but it doesn't moan. The neck
of the tree is stiff & cracks but it

never groans. A branch falls.
A kind of necessary surgery.

Even the weight of the page
is lighter without an appendix.

Even the moon grinds its teeth at night
& the man up the tree & the woman

in the clamshell. She grinds those pearly
whites to form a fine powder that she

smooths onto her face in the morning
after a night of overindulging in the sea.

Hate me because I'm beautiful! Not
for the extra bit of vibrato I've projected

around this note. At night even the piano
grinds its teeth. Even the earth shakes

in fear that it will break, as the
storm cries hard for a little while

like an overtired child with the saddest
eyes I've ever seen, her mind searching

as the sun, quick to snap the reins & stain
the stars in blood. Hers is a language of

water & wonderful for washing clean
the wreckage after a disaster. I watched her

like a screen as we began to bake. Time
passed & memories grazed, but mostly

I just watched her like a shy
soufflé that never rose.

From Pawn's Eye View

Try to remember from the beginning.
     What do you think that is on top of the night?
   A typewriter crawling away.
  Every feature in the cinema.
I'm interested in purchasing your vanity.
  For my own twisted purposes.
   Like a barter?
     Does it come with drawers built in?
       Steeped in pun.
Those smile lines are quite becoming.
  The bobby pins fixing my lips back.
   I'm sick of those bulimics & their optimism.
    I wear long, dangling earrings in spite of the fact.
    I'm always getting slapped in the eye on street corners.
      No penny in this city is lucky.
You can call a success a sputtering thing.
  But what would I be?
You can call an apple anything you'd like.
  Except for Japan.
A man, a woman, or a pot-bellied pig.
  The latter seems appealing.
Who needs politics?
  The butcher, the baker, the candlestick maker.
   Calling out to you.
    I love that confectionary body you made.
    You should see the body out of meat.
    Like a skeleton?
     Whose windchime is that?
   Duchamp's geometry book blowing in the wind.
I'm always getting slapped in the eye on street corners.
  I believe the pages are a little loose.
      That's your opinion.
Too many refined women here tonight.
   Too many balls in the game.
  That's your opinion.

Which one?

What do you think that is on top of the knight?

Why don't you rub those balls all over my heart?

But what would I be?

Every face you saw today.

Steeped in pun.

In purple Pashmina scarf & blazer.

Leroy, the Chinatown fish market cop.

With a passion for fish.

I was a psychic child.

Megaphone between my thighs.

Calling out to you.

You will love someone.

With a passion for fish.

You will meet someone.

Which one?

I like girls like that.

For my own twisted purposes.

Like a fleshy machine descending a staircase.

Steeped in allusion.

A typewriter crawling away.

The ladder seems appealing.

I believe the pages are a little loose.

Like a skeleton?

I like girls like that.

Steeped in illusion.

Peek over foot ache for love making wild slit baby.

Nothing like what it once was when you meant it.

Except for Japan.

More mistakes than I can count.

Try to remember from the beginning.

Every face you saw today.

Every feature in the cinema.

If You Saw, There Will Be Sawdust

I have done something that will confuse us.
It's shaped a bit like a train moving both ways,
closer to itself, a crumpled bridge,
a badly wrapped gift.
There is something inside. A bird cage
could stand for a home, but it is on its side.
Together we lie, your wing on my head, &
all this has been held. I have never
been terrified of a cockroach. This moving
both ways, not a sickness of seas. It is the raised
muscle in the neck like an implant. It is my breasts
with the lights out, or a tiny lamp & the dog
hairs all over us I hardly notice,
& the man that is a stiff
drink in the morning that I do,
& he is not you,
& he is not him & I
am not me, nor her & we three
are alone together in the bed of the earth.
It is so quiet I make smallish sniffing sounds.
I need you so badly it sickens the woods. You were inside
the belly of the tree. You are inside me.

The Tale of an Invisible Woman
Will Never Vanish

It will tiptoe about the house & clear its throat with a wariness
of sound. We cannot be star-crossed or crossed-off in nightgowns
of flesh! Those bones do not bring out the whites of your eyes,
or mine; they bring the bones out—your bone & my bone, each
heavy word, rolling around on the oak, bruising itself, heavier
than the fat lady herself, I'm always hitting notes before their
time. As an elephant I never forgot *The History of the Lake
Cannot Drown* & I'd cut off my trunk to give you a stump
on which to sit & rest your weary bones. For who am I
to deprive my love of an absence so vanishing it glows?
It's the tale of an invisible woman & the tale alone
that must offer up its obscurity, like a goat throat, I
don't have to remind you: there is a father up there
on the mountain for whom it is more than a throat.

Once He Left Me for the Lake

Once, & with an angry wafture of his hand,
we were dismissed, the daughters of
air; in our heads, we were prettier
than the tragic masks, crowns of cypress.
Haven't you got anything better
to wear than that cast? She thought
it would look better with his
name on it & signed the gauze
away to the river, my suitor, who
took three forms to ask me
of my father: a bull, a snake, a man
with an ox-like face. I have been
feeding him since the day I was born
from the ground, sort of an aquifer,
sort of awkward, I was wounded. I
didn't know myrrh from cassia,
nightshade from nightingale, I fed him—
I am wounded!—a shout leaped
from abroad, an impatient throng
rushed along his edges while overhead,
a sky of troubled grey & beyond, a lake.

Interlude in a Set of Jangling Keys

In this version, she wears his keys around
her hips like a bell
to ward off beasts—cool
calm & collected as a lake. She carries
herself through the landscape with all
the courage in the world
& every ounce of grace—so much so that
the rest of us walk around for days in circles
indecisive, irresponsible
& utterly graceless—sweating
our eyelashes off. Meanwhile, the grass
comes up around the rim
of the lake & frogs gather—almost
as if a fight were about
to break out on the surface, or the water
belonged to the pools
in the eyes of a Hollywood starlet, summoning
each one of nature's most vile
intruders & the power
to surmount them.

The Waters Broke

My god, she was stunning—
the onlookers buzzing
with osculations, her strawberry throat,
& plum of a tongue, punctuating
the earth, tricking lightning, throwing
sheep. I had exactly seven
girls in my trembling hands,
I dropped them & soon, everywhere
men were gesticulating, a woman
fainted, sesame in her drawers.
My own soul split
into seven whores, each one
crying, "More, sir!"
More.

Entr'acte

This section is completely unspeakable
because it is written in a whorish language.
Were I a lady of the night, I could read it
aloud. Perhaps I am
in a miniature replica of Saint-Sulpice,
where Our Lady sleeps.
Were I a dream, she would live
inside of me. But I am not
a dream. I am solid as a book & I throw
a shadow upon the wall like a fit
because I am a real woman
with the scars to prove it. I was 22
when I learned the word whore
could penetrate you better than most whores.
The word speaks to me because
it is thrown at me & it cuts
right through me, but I cannot
say it aloud until I admit
I am a whore. I cannot
replicate the shade of blue he wore
or the recipe for a disaster. Not the body
of another but the dream of her
clears the way to the greener side
like an eager toddler. Ours
might have been a lark. Holding a baby
bird in the hand is a wonderful art.

Lament in a Fixed Key

The stars are out, the money's terrible,
& the spring is boiling over.

What's a girl to do when she washes up?

> What anything else would do.
> Mark the shoreline.

I Keep Copies of This Question
in Color & in Black & White

For some time, her ship had been moving
in the direction of a star, but then

the breeze brought a droplet
in a gently rotating column

of air, like a twister but more
tender, softly turning her

towards a new way of life
without her even noticing

the curve. Suddenly, undressed
up to her hips, instead

of starring in the newest epic
Western produced by the darlings

of Tinseltown, her world
became the West—wild, treacherous

& blazing—scorched by the absence
of structures that might

actually uphold a civilization's
longevity. How did the ghost

towns foreshadow the currents
of chaos & mourning that are now

running through our ghostly cities
like waves of an outbreak?

The dust masks, the fever, the trash
in the river, glistening with flecks

of gold, a sunset reflected
in oil & suddenly on fire, a truck

mixed cement—its destiny
manifest. For centuries looking down,

she wondered who invented that glue,
which seemed to hold everything

together. Now, pressing her
fingers into glass, she could

look it up & feel the
cracks—tangerine beams

bounced off the buildings
& streets, poked through stray clouds

like strands of hair, evidence
that god just might be a woman

who prefers humanity a little
burnt around the edges,

whose back has been broken,
& she might be faulted as

the caramelized pavement
we walk, its bonds

ancient, far older than the West.
So many unpaved trails guided

that breeze & the concrete
here, cracking in anguish.

Apart at the Seams

I am the jasmine wafting down the spirit of the stairs.
I *am* the jasmine wafting down the spirit of the stairs!
Every dot of static is for me. Every stench.
Every piece of stucco on the houseboat!

I cannot say that I am *not* the heiress to a Rothschild,
inheriting pregnancy after pregnancy.
Can't you see that I *am* Mnemosyne?
I am the hemlock!

I am a black stone, smooth & round,
disparaged & abandoned by black plastic buttons,
squares inside of triangles, how can this be?
& everyone skips over me, across that great body...

But I know I am the frog empress. Kiss me!
Bend me back & pivot.
I am the unifying thread that runs through
the terrible fragments of radio segments & the film pieces & the deco
    pieces
& the excerpts of novels & their dying words
& the sound & picture would collide in time,
but they do not. No,

I am the silver dubbing over silence,
a student of the moment,
a minute emptier than rain...
Turn off the camera!

My subjects are the only ones to blame.
The jasmine enters the way they
left me, through the back door,
your manner precedes you no more
an emotional cure than the dark.

Like an Altar, or Minimalism

Night is never night enough.
Morning could be more morning.
Fell asleep with the TV, Janet Jackson
works her way into your dream. I can't remember
holding information in my head. I don't remember
what it was like before
there were lists in the clouds, entire
atlases in our eyes, the core of the earth.
This morning I discovered meditation
is molten, more lit than literature. It's true.
I am failing to speak the language
but I know now it is possible
to answer that calling towards
gravity. Dabbling in sincerity is not
the same as committing yourself
to one person. Everyone in the boxed
backyard seems to want boundlessness, life
without end. What if a boundary is
a promise? What if a limit gives it form?
What if a limit is a form of faith?
What about the neighborhood?
Is it safe? & how can I say? What
is the connection between rhythm
& libido, poetry & money, a dream
& a memory & a language & the lyricism
of matter, the warmth of the park bench
conducting sunlight in the square,
the square itself, "it will be great to see you" versus
"I can't wait to see you." If rhythm is the chart
of a temperament & you need some good, deep
diction in your life & poetry is uncounterfeiting,
uncounterfeitable, indefatigable, then why
do Rilke & I dream we are sculptors instead?
The principles of design do not apply

to death. Repetition is appealing to the eye
& yet we cut the fat. I wouldn't want to
make things awkward for you
by expressing my feelings about that.

It Was Enough for Us Just to Keep It Clean

There is too much dust in the air.
The slightest breeze & it's
back: it's rubbing its back
upon the marble tabletop & even
in the cracks of the wing-
backed chair, its beveled
arms. A wonderful dexterity, grace
in her hands like silver dragonflies,
weaving over one another, bringing life
to lace: white, ivory, lilac. It
is a heavenly palace. Who
will clean it?
      Some intruders
find their way into the south
wing of your house, & you let them
stay, never say hello, you never
leave your library anyway.
When you return to the spring
from which you were fed, from
whence you came & went &
returned, there is a man there now,
the water runs faster, you will be
like the water, you will not stop
for him in his black hat.
                        He
follows you, asks if you are
a pupil of St. John. Of course
you are a pupil of literally
everything around but say, "No."
He must stop so that the rest
of us can keep going. The water
is roaring now, the water is rising,
the dragonflies descend upon her hands
as if she were the water itself. There
is nothing one can do about love

but express it as often as possible.
There is nothing one can do
about beauty but make something
of it.
    Her father, the heavens
themselves, old & grey, bearded
as clouds, would tell her
she never earned it. Gifts
would be given to her, opportunities
would be presented but she
didn't deserve any of it
more than the next goddess
if she didn't bear children, if
she didn't return to the spring or leave
the library & stop. Is there any
palace a woman can enter
when she is afraid to fail?
One can reread a book, but once
the table has been set
or a headstone placed
you can't do it over again,
it's some kind of disgrace.

Tell It to the Doctor, Tell It to the Wind

If she had a heart, this is where it would live: the waterfall
spitting lightly on her face like a lover, the stones

bathing themselves in the open air
like Roman queens, smoothing out their skin.

Around her, the grass had tired itself of growing,
slumped against a shrub & fell asleep. Meanwhile, the buds

continued to push themselves out of their beds
like good mothers, so early, so young.

What a shame that time passes,
that spells break, that we get old

& mean & die & everything
good goes flying away. Wisdom

is so often overlooked, but put
the most familiar maxim in a new dress, mount her

on marble, & she will become an object of your
obsession: a goddess, stepping from peak to peak,

never planting her feet but on a mountain. Even
in wilderness, the imagination dominates, domesticates

its keeper but in a spirit palace. I dwell
in a many-colored cottage on the edge of the world.

Sometimes I am ashamed to breathe,
the sound & force of the need, so vulnerable am I

to the elements. A stroke of his lightning in the distance
& she becomes a poor, thin ghost of herself with a

twittering voice like a bat & no power to burn
with feeling. In my dreams I am armed

with scars, I can taste the iron-rich blood
moon in my mouth, & the gods still see me

as a flower? Delicate, uprooted, a muse is
not supposed to communicate in poetry but purely

through inspiration & a solid pout. Other times,
all of nature appears to her as if it were

nothing but a human in disguise, so well do the waterfall,
stone, grass & bud communicate our predicament.

Why Punish the Water for What It Needs

A green screen is no substitute for greenery.
Nature is nurturing, as is the solitude found
by the light of an almost-new moon. Satellites
are preferable to vultures—true. Seclusion of
the interior is a symptom of the new personality
disorder enforced by some states. On the upside, a soul
sickness can metastasize into money, celebrity, or
it dissolves into a clear broth with absolutely no value
to anyone, but for the stone we must believe in
because it came from the earth. She sits by a creek,
keeping six feet from her body, but the water
gets to go into town. What if we made a synthetic
saliva, exterior to the body? Droplets projecting
the future of medicine, as an organic tear
descends from her head on a mountaintop, outside
the ruin, it streams down her temple while
she ascends the wall of an ancient city, her hands
outstretched to the heavens in search of a
signal, so she can send proof of her ripening
patent on this hot new silver screen phenomenon
in which no one is allowed to go outside. She
could sue any one of us but has chosen
to settle like so many leaves in fall.

Only Light Where the Leaves Once Were

Truth, marrow, stone, & consequence.
She didn't earn a dime of it. The light,
hammering down on the desert
from the opposite side of your
expectations as the morning shifts
to afternoon. His hat tilted low
over one eye, he was practically debonair
in his exhaustion, drunk on the feather
in his cap. She asked
who gave it to him.
Once she'd skinny-dipped with some
kind of demigod
& his daughter. She found a dog
in the water & the word
for *family* was born.
She wanted to eat the lilies, be filled & floating
on the water like a body.
I can see her, sun-drenched
& precise & yet we have never met.
Love is a mystery that way,
more civil than any city, like a pilgrim
who reaches her destination
& cannot bear to stop.

Nothingland

Enter the landscape like
a bride when they gasp
assume it is your beauty
they are gasping at
when they cry pretend
it is your love
entering
the gorge like a groom
& you wait
for a long time
for the river to rush into you
on the bluffs
above the crag
of your soul
I am trying to capture
the magic of discovering
a pomegranate tree
where there was none
I am trying to give up
the notion of likeness
altogether I laid down
in the lagoon
like a straight flush
like a child bride
so baroque
she was the end of art
flaunting & squandering
its resources
now she keeps
a little blue dream on a shelf
like a bottle of brandy
visions of the infernal
feminine surging inside
you drove a painting
of a bright blue truck

through a hail storm
in my head now my heart
is a canoe in the middle of a lake
with no paddles
with nothing commercial
in her appearance
she was still a gleaming
toy of history
a luxury of literature
the voices of two men
chattering ominously in the distance
the echoes made tantalizing
by their shortcomings.
Who are you
when no one is watching?
How is a canyon
like a writing desk?
They both blow smoke.
Oh gentle fire
I am waiting to be blown
in some direction the way
the shadow of the shower
head at work
resembles a jellyfish
so too does my own head
work somewhat generically
she grew weary
of preparation
& connection
& illustration
of trying to screw up
the courage to fall
into his soft funereal hands
it's all a surface
grief so shallow
you might enjoy it in time
I hope to think

aphoristically
aristocratically
Dear me, am I walking?
I suppose I must be
I am learning
to be lively
to stimulate
my appetite
how did I come
to such a deep knowledge
of pleasure?
The Greeks
called an unmarried
woman an anecdote
the definition of which
was not yet set
in print she was about to draw
the lines out on her thighs
& on the sheets
& multiply & divide herself
by a broad-chested body
of water by a stroke
of exquisite simplicity
& singleness
of heart she wandered
until a honey-colored moon
appeared overhead

My That Was Fine & Then She Died

The pain I feel now is more sophisticated
than that old pain. If it burns, it burns up.
It is paper. The little girl in my dream & her skirt
is a lark. It can't even cover the check!
In default of wealth, one must have a *raison d'être*.
Is it too soon to say that I love you? Too soon
to know much. How do I find out?
Many years together in a bed
growing further. I need a lark
upon which I may focus my obsession.
Wind chimes alight on the shoulders of sirens
calling from the beach of my soul
Did somebody make love to me last night? I
have no one to tell of my drunkenness, despair
& the joy pressed out of me, cold
as an olive. I don't care to watch you
perform some enthusiasm. My performance
is a habit. I just miss you like a needle
misses the thread, the vein, I missed
the vein & died. I miss you like death
misses the unknown. Remember the
possibilities? Plagiarism can be
a collaboration, the pictures in the frames
are fakes. You can picture the frame, but
what does it contain? I don't think
we ever know the person we live with.
I have loved the person that I love
so much every single time but I can
tell you what I loved most about
my first was that he forgave me.
How do I create a form so wonderful
it need not contain a thing
& you will forgive me? I miss you,
Father, I miss my friends. I close
half my eyes, so you don't fall in.

Like gravity, there is nothing I can do
about it. I can't deny my girlhood
because a hood is a good way to cover
one's shame, oneself from the rain.
I want to look upon thee with the honesty
of an eye & never the hood around it.
The darkness creeps in along the edge
of my dream, allowing the stars to
shine. I want to take a picture of the sky,
but it is night. I like it when your
imagination comes out to play, babe, my
peppermint angel, when you asked me what
my Rome was like, that sleepy little hamlet.
I am no clown, I am perfection. Say it. My body
is American, strong, violent & full
of limitless potential & poetry
can be anything, the pages of my
girlhood left blank, it can be so beautiful
if you're not careful.

Afterword in the Allegory of a White Blanket & a Chandelier

Thanks to the times
in which she lived, there was
a layer of dust that coated
the keys, a covering

of questions like fog,
uncontrollably tearing up
the fabric of the living
room, the white night,

white woolen blanket,
stained by the blood of a
grape, rattlesnake, memory,
old fearful pattern

of words. Bread
helped with this process,
the flour dusting the crust
on her face. On the side

of a mountain, hundreds of
flying squirrels demonstrated
their boundless energy, practically
begging for more

responsibility. I would have
loved to give them the keys
to the palace, to recover
what was taken,

a diamond & her youth,
its blushing skin like a grape
& many wounds. One day,
suddenly savoring the scent

of her age like a loaf, she
rested & lay on the grass,
eyes closed, by the gate
preparing herself to leave.

When it opened, she walked
down a mountain, through a desert
to the sea. There is nothing more
valuable than water, she discovered—

not diamonds, nor data. There is
no window, mirror, or currency
like the face of a lake, but still,
like a vine, the facts & her figure

began to bear sweeter, riper
& more tender fruits. Science
became the crumb made
flesh & drop of wine made

paint, which is to say, if the wool
of the world is keeping you
too warm, seek an icy bath
in a glittering sea, oh light, oh god

of never understanding anything,
there is no chandelier like the stars
above, the flying squirrels
drinking moon milk.

Acknowledgments

Thank you to the editors of the following journals, magazines, and presses, who first published the poems mentioned below, often in earlier forms:

"As If I Hadn't Just Undressed Inside Her," "In Paintings We Appear in Forests in Threes," and "Even I, Who Have No Lover, Love" appeared in *Interim*.

"Why Punish the Water for What It Needs" appeared in *Bellevue Literary Review*.

"Just to Give You an Idea," "Below His Monocle," and "It Doesn't Hurt That She Is Beautiful" appeared in *Painted Bride Quarterly*.

"Nothingland" appeared in *Pouch*.

"The Waters Broke" appeared in *Fence*.

"It Was Enough for Us Just to Keep It Clean" appeared in *Elephant Journal*.

"Tossed to the Sky to Commemorate Her Death" and "Casting a Memory into the Cliff" appeared in *Bat City Review*.

"From What Abyss of Memory" and "A Beautiful Boyish Insouciance" appeared in *Prelude*.

"My That Was Fine & Then She Died" and "Before the Cold Bite of the Rattler" appeared in *Posit*.

"The Past Is Not the Past" appeared in *A Shadow Map: An Anthology by Survivors of Sexual Assault*, published by Civil Coping Mechanisms.

"Once He Left Me for the Lake" and "Only Light Where the Leaves Once Were" appeared in *Yes, Poetry*.

"Tell It to the Doctor, Tell It to the Wind" and "Like an Altar, or Minimalism" appeared in *Cosmonauts Avenue*.

"Sexual Misconduct," "The Graveyard," "My Mandolin," "From Pawn's Eye View," "If You Saw, There Will Be Sawdust," and "The Tale of an Invisible Woman Will Never Vanish" appeared in *In The Madame's Hat Box*, published by Dancing Girl Press.

About the Author

STEPHANIE BERGER is a poet, performer, experience designer, community organizer, and entrepreneur. She earned her BA in philosophy at the University of Southern California, received an MFA in poetry from the New School, and taught writing and film in the Department of English at Pace University. Berger is the founder and CEO of The Poetry Society of New York. Her writing has appeared in numerous publications, including *The New York Times* and *The New Yorker*.